UNMASKING THE STORY WITHIN

WRITING IN THE ROUGH

A Writer's Guidebook

Jan LaFave

Writing in the Rough, LLC

www.writingintherough.com

Writing in the Rough
A Writer's Guidebook

Unmasking the Story Within
Volume 1

Jump Starter Words and **Fantastic Words to Use with Dialogue** can be found in the English (United States) Dictionary, Thesaurus, or by searching the word name on the Internet.

Published by:
Writing in the Rough, LLC
www.writingintherough.com
Jan@writingintherough.com

Printed by CreateSpace, An Amazon.com Company

ISBN 978-0-9840233-3-2

Manufactured in the United States of America

How to use this book

FIRST YOU WILL NEED . . .

1. 9 pictures or photographs – 3 x 7 (3 inches high and 7 inches long) or smaller

2. Scissors to cut the pictures so they fit inside the box

3. Pencil or pen, crayons, colored pencils or markers

4. Tape or glue

If you don't have pictures or photographs, tape or glue, that's okay because you can draw the pictures using your imagination.

Step 1. Turn to page 6. Draw, tape or glue one of the 9 pictures into the rectangle ☐ at the top of the page.

Step 2. Look at the picture for 1 minute, longer if it's a really cool picture.

Step 3. Pick up your pen or pencil. Start with number 1. Read the questions and fill in the blanks with whatever pops into your head.

I CAN'T THINK OF ANYTHING TO WRITE!

Step 4. Don't panic. Help is on the next page. Look at the list of Jump Starter words and choose one you like. If you don't know what a word means, look it up in the dictionary.

Step 5. Once you have filled in all the blanks, turn the page. Illustrate **(that's a fancy word for draw)** your characters.

Step 6. Write dialogue between your characters. It's just like sending text messages back and forth. ⬚Character #1 ⬚Character #2 Check out page 96 for examples.

Step 7. Turn the page and write your story. Give your story a title.

Step 8. Turn the page and you'll Illustrate your story and jot down ideas for the next chapter.

TA DAH!!!!! You've just written your first story. Congratulations!!

Step 9. Now turn to the page at the **beginning** of your story that looks like this. Write the title of your story on the blank space. You wrote and illustrated the story, so your name goes on the WRITTEN BY and ILLUSTRATED BY lines.

Now use that **HUGE** square to draw a really cool picture about your story.

Step 10. Write the title of your story on the Table of Contents page.

Step 11. Fill the rest of the book with fantastic stories because you are . . .

Writing in the Rough! Are you ready? Turn to page 6 . . .

Table of Contents

Write story titles on the lines below.

CHAPTER 1

TITLE:_____

_____

WRITTEN BY: _____

ILLUSTRATED BY: _____

 GO TO NEXT PAGE ➡

6

Draw your own picture —or— choose a photograph from your phone or computer and print it —or— CUT A PICTURE FROM A MAGAZINE, NEWSPAPER, OR TRAVEL BROCHURE, **and glue or tape it into the box.**

Fill in the blanks. Write an answer to each prompt.

1. Get your senses involved. **Look at the picture.** Write down what you **See:** colors, shapes, sizes, people, and things. _____

_____

Put yourself in the picture.

Write down what you might **Hear:** _____ **Smell:** _____

Touch: _____ **Taste:** _____

I CAN'T THINK OF ANYTHING TO WRITE! Don't panic. **Help is on the next page** ⟶

2. Where is this place? Is it real or imaginary? **Location:** _____

3. When does this picture take place? **Time Period:** _____

4. What kind of day is it? **Weather:** _____

5. How does this picture make you feel? **Emotion:** _____

6. **Create** two **Characters**. Use the prompts to describe each one.

Character #1 Decide if your character will be a person, animal, or thing.

Body Frame: _____ Hair: _____

Eyes: _____ Complexion (face): _____

Teeth: _____ Nose: _____ Clothing: _____

_____

Personality: _____

Name: _____

GO TO NEXT PAGE ⟶

Character #2 <u>**Decide if your character will be a person, animal, or thing.**</u>

Body Frame: _____ Hair: _____

Eyes: _____ Complexion (face): _____

Teeth: _____ Nose: _____ Clothing: _____

_____

Personality: _____

Name: _____

7. Make up a **Problem** within the picture. What is the problem? What is happening to the

characters? _____

_____

8. What is the **Solution** to the problem? _____

_____

Need Help?	Oops! I want to use one of the words, but I don't know what it means.
Use a Jump Starter word, if needed, to respond to the prompts.	Write the word you want to use. Look up the word in the dictionary and write down what it means.
Hear: pounding	_____
Smell: cheese	_____
Touch: flour	_____
Taste: dental floss	_____
Location: Outer Space	_____
Time Period: Stone Age	_____
Weather: solar eclipse	_____
Emotion: blissful	_____
Body Frame: tree, muscular	_____
Hair: Ducktail, shaved	_____
Eyes: stunned, worried	_____
Complexion (face): wrinkles, mole	_____
Teeth: squeaky-clean, stained	_____
Nose: aquiline, snub-nosed	_____
Clothing: mask, jacket	_____
Personality: live wire, snooping	_____
Problem: collapsed bridge	

GO TO NEXT PAGE ▶

8

Draw your characters.

Character #1

Character #2

 GO TO NEXT PAGE ➡

Write dialogue between your characters. What are they saying to each other?
<u>Write one sentence in each speech bubble.</u> See page 96 for examples of dialogue.

Character #1

Character #2

Character #1

Character #2

Character #1

Character #2

Character #1

Character #2

Character #1

Character #2

 GO TO NEXT PAGE ➡

10

Put it all together. Use your writing from pages 6-9 to write a short story. Describe the **Location**, **Time Period**, and **Weather**. Add details about the **Characters** and their **Problem**. Add some or all of the dialogue from page 9 to spice up your story. Finish the story by **Solving** the problem.

_____

_____

_____

_____

_____

_____

_____

_____

_____

Did you know . . .

when writing dialogue, the quotation marks go around the words like this?

"My dental floss disappeared during the solar eclipse!"

_____

_____

_____

_____

_____

_____

_____

_____

_____

_____

_____

 GO TO NEXT PAGE➡

GO TO NEXT PAGE ➡

_____

_____

_____

_____

_____

_____

_____

_____

_____

_____

_____

_____

_____

_____

_____

_____

_____

_____

_____

What would be a great title for this story? Write your title here. ↙

_____

Illustrate your story.

Beginning

Middle

End

 GO TO NEXT PAGE ➡

What else could happen to the characters?

Other story ideas

GO TO NEXT PAGE ➡

STOP

CONGRATULATIONS!

You have just finished writing Chapter 1

Now . . .

Go back to page 5. **Write the title of this story** on the line next to TITLE: _____. Then **write your name** next to WRITTEN BY: _____ and ILLUSTRATED BY: _____. Draw a picture in the box above the title that will show the reader what this chapter is about.

After you finish page 5, start the next chapter

GO TO NEXT PAGE ➡

CHAPTER 2

TITLE:_____

_____

WRITTEN BY: _____

ILLUSTRATED BY: _____

16

Draw your own picture —or— choose a photograph from your phone or computer and print it —or— CUT A PICTURE FROM A MAGAZINE, NEWSPAPER, OR TRAVEL BROCHURE, **and glue or tape it into the box.**

Fill in the blanks. Write an answer to each prompt.

1. Get your senses involved. **Look at the picture.** Write down what you **See:** colors, shapes, sizes, people, and things. _____

_____

Put yourself in the picture.

Write down what you might **Hear:** _____ **Smell:** _____

Touch: _____ **Taste:** _____

I CAN'T THINK OF ANYTHING TO WRITE! Don't panic. **Help is on the next page** ⟶

2. Where is this place? Is it real or imaginary? **Location:** _____

3. When does this picture take place? **Time Period:** _____

4. What kind of day is it? **Weather:** _____

5. How does this picture make you feel? **Emotion:** _____

6. **Create** two **Characters**. Use the prompts to describe each one.

Character #1 Decide if your character will be a person, animal, or thing.

Body Frame: _____ Hair: _____

Eyes: _____ Complexion (face): _____

Teeth: _____ Nose: _____ Clothing: _____

_____

Personality: _____

Name: _____

 GO TO NEXT PAGE ⟶

Character #2 <u>Decide if your character will be a person, animal, or thing.</u>

Body Frame: _____ Hair: _____

Eyes: _____ Complexion (face): _____

Teeth: _____ Nose: _____ Clothing: _____

_____

Personality: _____

Name: _____

7. Make up a **Problem** within the picture. What is the problem? What is happening to the characters? _____

_____

8. What is the **Solution** to the problem? _____

_____

Need Help? Use a Jump Starter word, if needed, to respond to the prompts.	Oops! I want to use one of the words, but I don't know what it means. Write the word you want to use. Look up the word in the dictionary and write down what it means.
Hear: fan-blowing air **Smell:** onions **Touch:** piano keys **Taste:** banana **Location:** creek **Time Period:** Middle Ages **Weather:** Nor'easter **Emotion:** motivated **Body Frame:** beanpole, roly-poly **Hair:** carrot top, gray **Eyes:** shocked, weepy **Complexion (face):** wart, glittery **Teeth:** yellow, broken **Nose:** congested, sphere-shaped **Clothing:** nightgown, uniform **Personality:** intelligent, spoiled **Problem:** lost in a forest	_____ _____ _____ _____ _____ _____ _____ _____ _____ _____ _____ _____ _____ _____ _____ _____

18

Draw your characters.

Character #1

Character #2

 GO TO NEXT PAGE ➡

Write dialogue between your characters. What are they saying to each other?
<u>Write one sentence in each speech bubble.</u> See page 96 for examples of dialogue.

Character #1

Character #2

Character #1

Character #2

Character #1

Character #2

Character #1

Character #2

Character #1

Character #2

 GO TO NEXT PAGE

20

Put it all together. Use your writing from pages 16-19 to write a short story. Describe the **Location**, **Time Period**, and **Weather**. Add details about the **Characters** and their **Problem**. Add some or all of the dialogue from page 19 to spice up your story. Finish the story by **Solving** the problem.

_____

_____

_____

_____

_____

_____

_____

_____

> *Did you know . . .*
>
> *all sentences begin with a capital letter?*
>
> **The** bear with the ratty hair ate an unripe banana.

_____

_____

_____

_____

_____

_____

_____

_____

_____

 GO TO NEXT PAGE ➡

_____

_____

_____

_____

_____

_____

_____

_____

_____

_____

_____

_____

_____

_____

_____

_____

_____

_____

_____

What would be a great title for this story? Write your title here.

_____

 GO TO NEXT PAGE ➡

Illustrate your story.

Beginning

Middle

End

What else could happen to the characters?

Other story ideas

 GO TO NEXT PAGE ➡

STOP

CONGRATULATIONS!

You have just finished writing Chapter 2

Now . . .

Go back to page 15. **Write the title of this story** on the line next to TITLE: ____. Then **write your name** next to WRITTEN BY: _____ and ILLUSTRATED BY: _____. Draw a picture in the box above the title that will show the reader what this chapter is about.

After you finish page 15, start the next chapter

 GO TO NEXT PAGE ➡

CHAPTER 3

TITLE:_____

_____

WRITTEN BY: _____

ILLUSTRATED BY: _____

26

Draw your own picture —or— choose a photograph from your phone or computer and print it —or— CUT A PICTURE FROM A MAGAZINE, NEWSPAPER, OR TRAVEL BROCHURE, **and glue or tape it into the box.**

Fill in the blanks. Write an answer to each prompt.

1. Get your senses involved. **Look at the picture.** Write down what you **See:** colors, shapes, sizes, people, and things. _____

_____

Put yourself in the picture.

Write down what you might **Hear:** _____ **Smell:** _____

Touch: _____ **Taste:** _____

I CAN'T THINK OF ANYTHING TO WRITE! Don't panic. **Help is on the next page** ⟶

2. Where is this place? Is it real or imaginary? **Location:** _____

3. When does this picture take place? **Time Period:** _____

4. What kind of day is it? **Weather:** _____

5. How does this picture make you feel? **Emotion:** _____

6. **Create** two **Characters**. Use the prompts to describe each one.

Character #1 Decide if your character will be a person, animal, or thing.

Body Frame: _____ Hair: _____

Eyes: _____ Complexion (face): _____

Teeth: _____ Nose: _____ Clothing: _____

_____

Personality: _____

Name: _____

 GO TO NEXT PAGE ⟶

Character #2 <u>Decide if your character will be a person, animal, or thing.</u>

Body Frame: _____ Hair: _____

Eyes: _____ Complexion (face): _____

Teeth: _____ Nose: _____ Clothing: _____

_____

Personality: _____

Name: _____

7. Make up a **Problem** within the picture. What is the problem? What is happening to the

characters? _____

_____

8. What is the **Solution** to the problem? _____

_____

Need Help? Use a Jump Starter word, if needed, to respond to the prompts.	Oops! I want to use one of the words, but I don't know what it means. Write the word you want to use. Look up the word in the dictionary and write down what it means.
Hear: chirping	_____
Smell: stinky feet	_____
Touch: soil	_____
Taste: burning	_____
Location: brain	_____
Time Period: long-ago	_____
Weather: typhoon	_____
Emotion: riveted	_____
Body Frame: apple-shaped, gorilla-like	_____
Hair: smooth, pigtails	_____
Eyes: scheming, watchful	_____
Complexion (face): sunburned, face cream	_____
Teeth: pristine, ridges	_____
Nose: plugged, curved	_____
Clothing: necklace, tiara	_____
Personality: insistent, encourager	_____
Problem: trapped in a floating bubble	_____

 GO TO NEXT PAGE

Draw your characters.

Character #1

Character #2

GO TO NEXT PAGE ➡

Write dialogue between your characters. What are they saying to each other? <u>Write one sentence in each speech bubble.</u> See page 96 for examples of dialogue.

Character #1

Character #2

Character #1

Character #2

Character #1

Character #2

Character #1

Character #2

Character #1

Character #2

GO TO NEXT PAGE ➡

30

Put it all together. Use your writing from pages 26-29 to write a short story. Describe the **Location**, **Time Period**, and **Weather**. Add details about the **Characters** and their **Problem**. Add some or all of the dialogue from page 29 to spice up your story. Finish the story by **Solving** the problem.

_____

_____

_____

_____

_____

_____

_____

_____

_____

Did you know . . .

sentences end with

a period (.)

an exclamation point (!)

or question mark (?)

_____

_____

_____

_____

_____

_____

_____

_____

_____

 GO TO NEXT PAGE ➡

_____

_____

_____

_____

_____

_____

_____

_____

_____

_____

_____

_____

_____

_____

_____

_____

_____

_____

What would be a great title for this story? Write your title here.

_____

 GO TO NEXT PAGE ➡

Illustrate your story.

Beginning

Middle

End

 GO TO NEXT PAGE➡

What else could happen to the characters?

Other story ideas

GO TO NEXT PAGE ➡

STOP

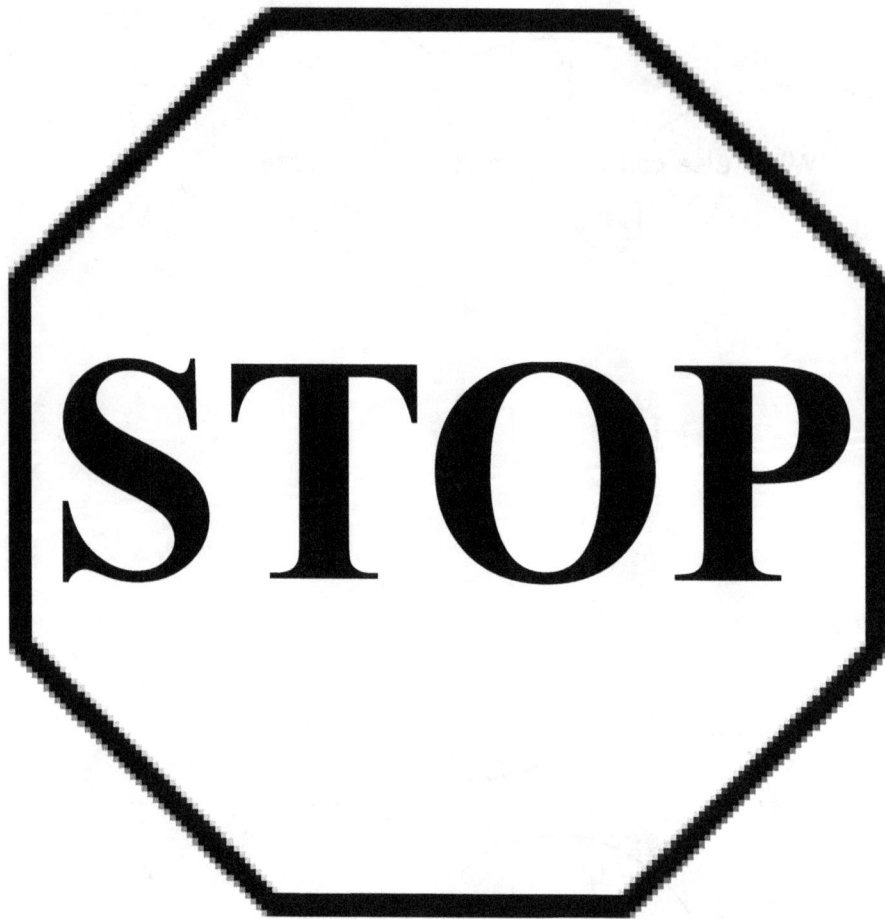

CONGRATULATIONS!

You have just finished writing Chapter 3

Now . . .

Go back to page 25. Write the title of this story on the line next to TITLE: _____. Then **write your name** next to WRITTEN BY: _____ and ILLUSTRATED BY: _____. Draw a picture in the box above the title that will show the reader what this chapter is about.

After you finish page 25, start the next chapter

GO TO NEXT PAGE ➡

CHAPTER 4

TITLE:_____

_____

WRITTEN BY: _____

ILLUSTRATED BY: _____

36

Draw your own picture —or— choose a photograph from your phone or computer and print it —or— cut A PICTURE FROM A MAGAZINE, NEWSPAPER, OR TRAVEL BROCHURE, **and glue or tape it into the box.**

Fill in the blanks. Write an answer to each prompt.

1. Get your senses involved. **Look at the picture.** Write down what you **See:** colors, shapes, sizes, people, and things. _____

_____

Put yourself in the picture.

Write down what you might **Hear:** _____ **Smell:** _____

Touch: _____ **Taste:** _____

I CAN'T THINK OF ANYTHING TO WRITE! Don't panic. **Help is on the next page** ⟶

2. Where is this place? Is it real or imaginary? **Location:** _____

3. When does this picture take place? **Time Period:** _____

4. What kind of day is it? **Weather:** _____

5. How does this picture make you feel? **Emotion:** _____

6. **Create** two **Characters.** Use the prompts to describe each one.

Character #1 Decide if your character will be a person, animal, or thing.

Body Frame: _____ Hair: _____

Eyes: _____ Complexion (face): _____

Teeth: _____ Nose: _____ Clothing: _____

_____

Personality: _____

Name: _____

GO TO NEXT PAGE ➡

Character #2 <u>Decide if your character will be a person, animal, or thing.</u>

Body Frame: _____ Hair: _____

Eyes: _____ Complexion (face): _____

Teeth: _____ Nose: _____ Clothing: _____

_____

Personality: _____

Name: _____

7. Make up a **Problem** within the picture. What is the problem? What is happening to the

characters? _____

_____

8. What is the **Solution** to the problem? _____

_____

Need Help? Use a Jump Starter word, if needed, to respond to the prompts.	Oops! I want to use one of the words, but I don't know what it means. Write the word you want to use. Look up the word in the dictionary and write down what it means.
Hear: radio	_____
Smell: sachet	_____
Touch: tree bark	_____
Taste: nutty	_____
Location: palace	_____
Time Period: New Millennium	_____
Weather: hailstorm	_____
Emotion: thankful	_____
Body Frame: glove, teapot	_____
Hair: braids, wavy	_____
Eyes: scared, surprised	_____
Complexion (face): sickly, face paint	_____
Teeth: wooden, decomposed	_____
Nose: snoring, diamond-shaped	_____
Clothing: mittens, suit of armor	_____
Personality: cheerful, hateful	_____
Problem: swallowed by a giant snake	_____

GO TO NEXT PAGE ➡

38

Draw your characters.

Character #1

Character #2

 GO TO NEXT PAGE ➡

Write dialogue between your characters. What are they saying to each other?
<u>Write one sentence in each speech bubble.</u> See page 96 for examples of dialogue.

Character #1

Character #2

Character #1

Character #2

Character #1

Character #2

Character #1

Character #2

Character #1

Character #2

GO TO NEXT PAGE ➡

40

Put it all together. Use your writing from pages 36-39 to write a short story. Describe the **Location**, **Time Period**, and **Weather**. Add details about the **Characters** and their **Problem**. Add some or all of the dialogue from page 39 to spice up your story. Finish the story by **Solving** the problem.

_____

_____

_____

_____

_____

_____

_____

_____

_____

> **Did you know . . .**
>
> **you can start a story with a question?**
>
> "Who took the old tattered book from my trunk?" croaked the man with the wiry hair.

_____

_____

_____

_____

_____

_____

_____

_____

_____

_____

_____

_____

_____

_____

_____

_____

_____

_____

_____

_____

_____

_____

_____

_____

_____

_____

_____

_____

What would be a great title for this story? Write your title here. ↓

_____

 GO TO NEXT PAGE ➡

Illustrate your story.

Beginning

Middle

End

 GO TO NEXT PAGE ➡

What else could happen to the characters?

Other story ideas

STOP

CONGRATULATIONS!

You have just finished writing Chapter 4

Now . . .

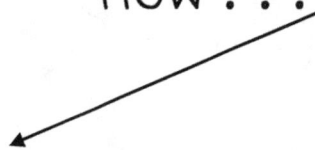

Go back to page 35. **Write the title of this story** on the line next to TITLE: ____. Then **write your name** next to WRITTEN BY: _____ and ILLUSTRATED BY: _____. Draw a picture in the box above the title that will show the reader what this chapter is about.

<u>After</u> you finish page 35, start the next chapter

GO TO NEXT PAGE ➡

CHAPTER 5

TITLE:_____

_____

WRITTEN BY: _____

ILLUSTRATED BY: _____

46

Draw your own picture —or— choose a photograph from your phone or computer and print it —or— CUT A PICTURE FROM A MAGAZINE, NEWSPAPER, OR TRAVEL BROCHURE, **and glue or tape it into the box.**

Fill in the blanks. Write an answer to each prompt.

1. Get your senses involved. **Look at the picture.** Write down what you **See:** colors, shapes, sizes, people, and things. _____

_____

Put yourself in the picture.

Write down what you might **Hear:** _____ **Smell:** _____

Touch: _____ **Taste:** _____

I CAN'T THINK OF ANYTHING TO WRITE! Don't panic. **Help is on the next page** ⟶

2. Where is this place? Is it real or imaginary? **Location:** _____

3. When does this picture take place? **Time Period:** _____

4. What kind of day is it? **Weather:** _____

5. How does this picture make you feel? **Emotion:** _____

6. **Create** two **Characters**. Use the prompts to describe each one.

Character #1 Decide if your character will be a person, animal, or thing.

Body Frame: _____ Hair: _____

Eyes: _____ Complexion (face): _____

Teeth: _____ Nose: _____ Clothing: _____

_____

Personality: _____

Name: _____

GO TO NEXT PAGE ⟶

Character #2 <u>Decide if your character will be a person, animal, or thing.</u>

Body Frame: _____ Hair: _____

Eyes: _____ Complexion (face): _____

Teeth: _____ Nose: _____ Clothing: _____

_____

Personality: _____

Name: _____

7. Make up a **Problem** within the picture. What is the problem? What is happening to the

characters? _____

_____

8. What is the **Solution** to the problem? _____

_____

Need Help? Use a 𝓙𝓾𝓶𝓹 𝓢𝓽𝓪𝓻𝓽𝓮𝓻 word, if needed, to respond to the prompts.	Oops! I want to use one of the words, but I don't know what it means. Write the word you want to use. Look up the word in the dictionary and write down what it means.
Hear: footsteps	_____
Smell: nail polish	_____
Touch: stair railing	_____
Taste: chewy	_____
Location: citadel	_____
Time Period: 10 minutes ago	_____
Weather: volcanic eruption	_____
Emotion: surprised	_____
Body Frame: wiry, box	_____
Hair: choppy layers, Pageboy	_____
Eyes: sad, startled	_____
Complexion (face): shiny, lines	_____
Teeth: gilded, dull	_____
Nose: bubble, frostbitten	_____
Clothing: in-line skates, spacesuit	_____
Personality: gossip, reclusive	_____
Problem: no electricity	_____

GO TO NEXT PAGE ➡

Draw your characters.

Character #1

Character #2

 GO TO NEXT PAGE ➡

Write dialogue between your characters. What are they saying to each other?
<u>Write one sentence in each speech bubble.</u> See page 96 for examples of dialogue.

Character #1

Character #2

Character #1

Character #2

Character #1

Character #2

Character #1

Character #2

Character #1

Character #2

GO TO NEXT PAGE ➡

50

Put it all together. Use your writing from pages 46-49 to write a short story. Describe the **Location**, **Time Period**, and **Weather**. Add details about the **Characters** and their **Problem**. Add some or all of the dialogue from page 49 to spice up your story. Finish the story by **Solving** the problem.

_____

_____

_____

_____

_____

_____

_____

_____

_____

Did you know . . .	_____
you can start a story by changing something that is real into something that isn't real?	_____
	_____
	_____
I sipped the sour drink through the ends of my spiked hair. I wasn't always this way. It all started when . . .	_____
	_____
	_____

_____

_____

_____

 GO TO NEXT PAGE ➡

_____

_____

_____

_____

_____

_____

_____

_____

_____

_____

_____

_____

_____

_____

_____

_____

_____

_____

What would be a great title for this story? Write your title here.

_____

 GO TO NEXT PAGE ▶

Illustrate your story.

Beginning

Middle

End

 GO TO NEXT PAGE ➡

What else could happen to the characters?

Other story ideas

GO TO NEXT PAGE ➡

STOP

CONGRATULATIONS!

You have just finished writing Chapter 5

Now . . .

Go back to page 45. Write the title of this story on the line next to TITLE: _____. Then **write your name** next to WRITTEN BY: _____ and ILLUSTRATED BY: _____. Draw a picture in the box above the title that will show the reader what this chapter is about.

After you finish page 45, start the next chapter

GO TO NEXT PAGE ➡

CHAPTER 6

TITLE:_____

_____

WRITTEN BY: _____

ILLUSTRATED BY: _____

 GO TO NEXT PAGE

56

Draw your own picture —or— choose a photograph from your phone or computer and print it —or— CUT A PICTURE FROM A MAGAZINE, NEWSPAPER, OR TRAVEL BROCHURE, **and glue or tape it into the box.**

[ ]

Fill in the blanks. Write an answer to each prompt.

1. Get your senses involved. **Look at the picture.** Write down what you **See:** colors, shapes, sizes, people, and things. _____

_____

Put yourself in the picture.

Write down what you might **Hear:** _____ **Smell:** _____

Touch: _____ **Taste:** _____

I CAN'T THINK OF ANYTHING TO WRITE! Don't panic. **Help is on the next page** ⟶

2. Where is this place? Is it real or imaginary? **Location:** _____

3. When does this picture take place? **Time Period:** _____

4. What kind of day is it? **Weather:** _____

5. How does this picture make you feel? **Emotion:** _____

6. **Create** two **Characters**. Use the prompts to describe each one.

Character #1 Decide if your character will be a person, animal, or thing.

Body Frame: _____ Hair: _____

Eyes: _____ Complexion (face): _____

Teeth: _____ Nose: _____ Clothing: _____

_____

Personality: _____

Name: _____

GO TO NEXT PAGE ⟶

Character #2 <u>Decide if your character will be a person, animal, or thing.</u>

Body Frame: _____ Hair: _____

Eyes: _____ Complexion (face): _____

Teeth: _____ Nose: _____ Clothing: _____

_____

Personality: _____

Name: _____

7. Make up a **Problem** within the picture. What is the problem? What is happening to the characters? _____

_____

8. What is the **Solution** to the problem? _____

_____

Need Help?	Oops! I want to use one of the words, but I don't know what it means.
Use a *Jump Starter* word, if needed, to respond to the prompts.	Write the word you want to use. Look up the word in the dictionary and write down what it means.

Hear: leaky faucet

Smell: fresh air

Touch: mud

Taste: melting chocolate

Location: bottom of the sea

Time Period: 1980s

Weather: drought

Emotion: troubled

Body Frame: tortoise-shell, potato

Hair: spiked, curly

Eyes: inattentive, staring

Complexion (face): sallow, make-up

Teeth: radiant, black

Nose: swollen, freckles

Clothing: housecoat, sandals

Personality: glum, precocious

Problem: tangled in a spiderweb

GO TO NEXT PAGE ➡

58

Draw your characters.

Character #1

Character #2

 GO TO NEXT PAGE ➡

Write dialogue between your characters. What are they saying to each other?
<u>Write one sentence in each speech bubble.</u> See page 96 for examples of dialogue.

Character #1

Character #2

Character #1

Character #2

Character #1

Character #2

Character #1

Character #2

Character #1

Character #2

 GO TO NEXT PAGE ➡

60

Put it all together. Use your writing from pages 56-59 to write a short story. Describe the **Location**, **Time Period**, and **Weather**. Add details about the **Characters** and their **Problem**. Add some or all of the dialogue from page 59 to spice up your story. Finish the story by **Solving** the problem.

_____

_____

_____

_____

_____

_____

_____

_____

_____

Did you know . . .

you can start a story with the ending?

Exhilarated the hunt was finally over, I scooped the gold coins into my satchel and headed home. I pondered the day I found the old crinkled map. I was cleaning . . .

_____

_____

_____

_____

_____

_____

_____

_____

_____

_____

 GO TO NEXT PAGE ➡

_____

_____

_____

_____

_____

_____

_____

_____

_____

_____

_____

_____

_____

_____

_____

_____

_____

_____

What would be a great title for this story? Write your title here.

_____

GO TO NEXT PAGE ➡

Illustrate your story.

Beginning

Middle

End

 GO TO NEXT PAGE ➡

What else could happen to the characters?

Other story ideas

 GO TO NEXT PAGE ➡

STOP

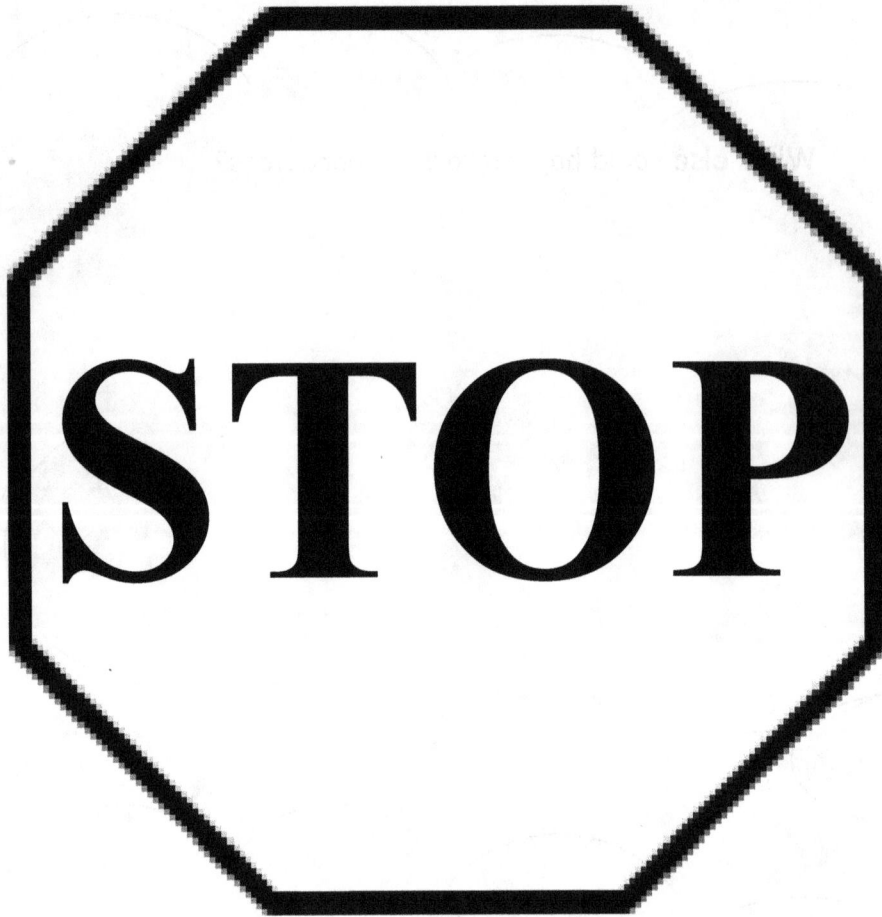

CONGRATULATIONS!

You have just finished writing Chapter 6

Now . . .

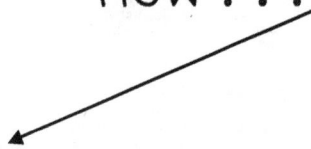

Go back to page 55. **Write the title of this story** on the line next to TITLE: _____. Then **write your name** next to WRITTEN BY: _____ and ILLUSTRATED BY: _____. Draw a picture in the box above the title that will show the reader what this chapter is about.

After you finish page 55, start the next chapter

 GO TO NEXT PAGE →

CHAPTER 7

TITLE:_____

_____

WRITTEN BY: _____

ILLUSTRATED BY: _____

66

Draw your own picture —or— choose a photograph from your phone or computer and print it —or— CUT A PICTURE FROM A MAGAZINE, NEWSPAPER, OR TRAVEL BROCHURE, **and glue or tape it into the box.**

Fill in the blanks. Write an answer to each prompt.

1. Get your senses involved. **Look at the picture.** Write down what you **See:** colors, shapes, sizes, people, and things. _____

_____

Put yourself in the picture.

Write down what you might **Hear:** _____ **Smell:** _____

Touch: _____ **Taste:** _____

I CAN'T THINK OF ANYTHING TO WRITE! Don't panic. **Help is on the next page** ⟶

2. Where is this place? Is it real or imaginary? **Location:** _____

3. When does this picture take place? **Time Period:** _____

4. What kind of day is it? **Weather:** _____

5. How does this picture make you feel? **Emotion:** _____

6. **Create** two **Characters**. Use the prompts to describe each one.

Character #1 Decide if your character will be a person, animal, or thing.

Body Frame: _____ Hair: _____

Eyes: _____ Complexion (face): _____

Teeth: _____ Nose: _____ Clothing: _____

_____

Personality: _____

Name: _____

GO TO NEXT PAGE ⟶

Character #2 <u>Decide if your character will be a person, animal, or thing.</u>

Body Frame: _____ Hair: _____

Eyes: _____ Complexion (face): _____

Teeth: _____ Nose: _____ Clothing: _____

_____

Personality: _____

Name: _____

7. Make up a **Problem** within the picture. What is the problem? What is happening to the characters? _____

_____

8. What is the **Solution** to the problem? _____

_____

Need Help? Use a Jump Starter word, if needed, to respond to the prompts.	Oops! I want to use one of the words, but I don't know what it means. Write the word you want to use. Look up the word in the dictionary and write down what it means.
Hear: sneezing	_____
Smell: fish	_____
Touch: leather	_____
Taste: sweet	_____
Location: moon	_____
Time Period: 1960s	_____
Weather: downpour	_____
Emotion: fortunate	_____
Body Frame: blob, flower	_____
Hair: blonde, hairpiece	_____
Eyes: cry your eyes out, dark	_____
Complexion (face): purple, blushing	_____
Teeth: flashing, gigantic	_____
Nose: blister, wet	_____
Clothing: headscarf, shawl	_____
Personality: friendly, pompous	_____
Problem: shrunk to the size of an ant	_____

GO TO NEXT PAGE

68

Draw your characters.

Character #1

Character #2

 GO TO NEXT PAGE ➡

Write dialogue between your characters. What are they saying to each other?
<u>Write one sentence in each speech bubble.</u> See page 96 for examples of dialogue.

Character #1

Character #2

Character #1

Character #2

Character #1

Character #2

Character #1

Character #2

Character #1

Character #2

 GO TO NEXT PAGE ➡

70

Put it all together. Use your writing from pages 66-69 to write a short story. Describe the **Location**, **Time Period**, and **Weather**. Add details about the **Characters** and their **Problem**. Add some or all of the dialogue from page 69 to spice up your story. Finish the story by **Solving** the problem.

_____

_____

_____

_____

_____

_____

_____

_____

Did you know . . .

you should start a new paragraph when there is a change in time, place, topic, or person?

_____

_____

_____

_____

_____

_____

_____

_____

_____

_____

 GO TO NEXT PAGE ➡

_____

_____

_____

_____

_____

_____

_____

_____

_____

_____

_____

_____

_____

_____

_____

_____

_____

_____

_____

_____

_____

_____

What would be a great title for this story? Write your title here.

_____

Illustrate your story.

Beginning

Middle

End

 GO TO NEXT PAGE ➡

What else could happen to the characters?

Other story ideas

STOP

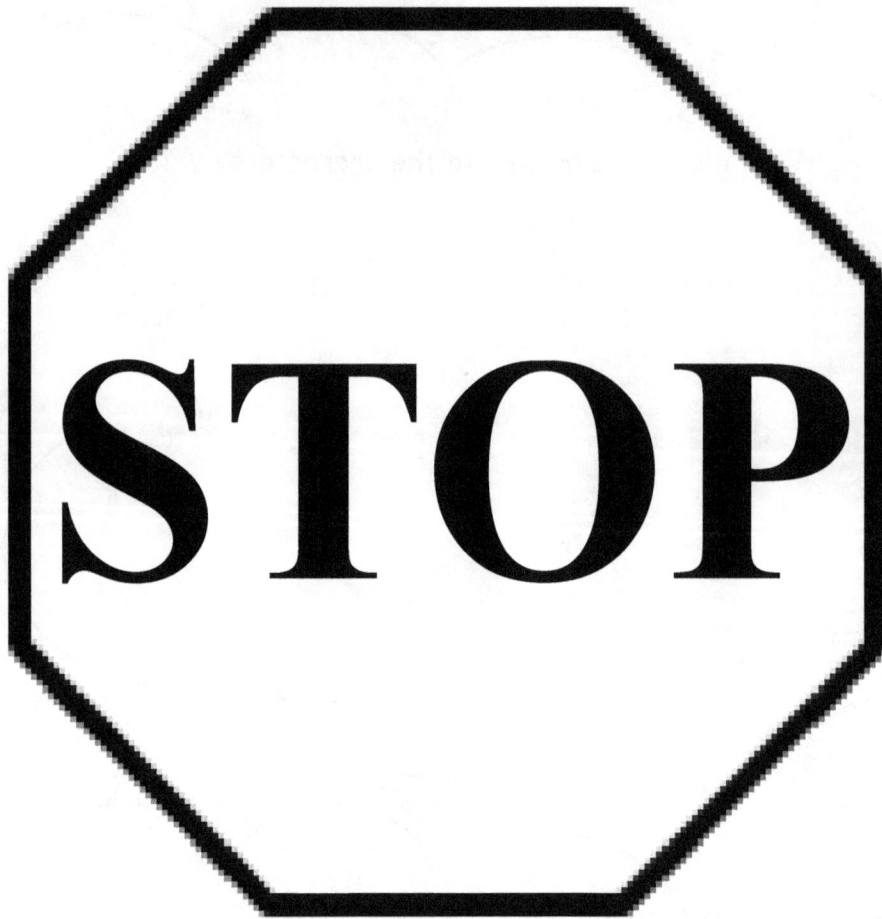

CONGRATULATIONS!

You have just finished writing Chapter 7

Now . . .

Go back to page 65. **Write the title of this story** on the line next to TITLE: _____. Then **write your name** next to WRITTEN BY: _____ and ILLUSTRATED BY: _____. Draw a picture in the box above the title that will show the reader what this chapter is about.

After you finish page 65, start the next chapter

GO TO NEXT PAGE ➡

CHAPTER 8

TITLE:_____

_____

WRITTEN BY: _____

ILLUSTRATED BY: _____

Draw your own picture —or— choose a photograph from your phone or computer and print it —or— CUT A PICTURE FROM A MAGAZINE, NEWSPAPER, OR TRAVEL BROCHURE, and glue or tape it into the box.

Fill in the blanks. Write an answer to each prompt.

1. Get your senses involved. **Look at the picture.** Write down what you **See:** colors, shapes, sizes, people, and things. _____

_____

Put yourself in the picture.

Write down what you might **Hear:** _____ **Smell:** _____

Touch: _____ **Taste:** _____

I CAN'T THINK OF ANYTHING TO WRITE! Don't panic. **Help is on the next page** ⟶

2. Where is this place? Is it real or imaginary? **Location**: _____

3. When does this picture take place? **Time Period**: _____

4. What kind of day is it? **Weather**: _____

5. How does this picture make you feel? **Emotion**: _____

6. **Create** two **Characters**. Use the prompts to describe each one.

Character #1 Decide if your character will be a person, animal, or thing.

Body Frame: _____ Hair: _____

Eyes: _____ Complexion (face): _____

Teeth: _____ Nose: _____ Clothing: _____

_____

Personality: _____

Name: _____

 GO TO NEXT PAGE ⟶

Character #2 <u>**Decide if your character will be a person, animal, or thing.**</u>

Body Frame: _____ Hair: _____

Eyes: _____ Complexion (face): _____

Teeth: _____ Nose: _____ Clothing: _____

_____

Personality: _____

Name: _____

7. Make up a **Problem** within the picture. What is the problem? What is happening to the characters? _____

_____

8. What is the **Solution** to the problem? _____

_____

Need Help? Use a Jump Starter word, if needed, to respond to the prompts.	Oops! I want to use one of the words, but I don't know what it means. Write the word you want to use. Look up the word in the dictionary and write down what it means.
Hear: loudspeaker	_____
Smell: car exhaust	_____
Touch: sludge	_____
Taste: crackers	_____
Location: solar system	_____
Time Period: midnight	_____
Weather: tsunami	_____
Emotion: jovial	_____
Body Frame: small, pencil	_____
Hair: black, golden	_____
Eyes: attentive, pinkeye	_____
Complexion (face): rash, muddy	_____
Teeth: blanched, seashells	_____
Nose: pointed, warm	_____
Clothing: fedora, sarong	_____
Personality: curious, outgoing	_____
Problem: wrong turn	_____

GO TO NEXT PAGE ▶

Draw your characters.

Character #1

Character #2

 GO TO NEXT PAGE ➡

Write dialogue between your characters. What are they saying to each other? <u>Write one sentence in each speech bubble.</u> See page 96 for examples of dialogue.

Character #1

Character #2

Character #1

Character #2

Character #1

Character #2

Character #1

Character #2

Character #1

Character #2

 GO TO NEXT PAGE ➡

80

Put it all together. Use your writing from pages 76-79 to write a short story. Describe the **Location**, **Time Period**, and **Weather**. Add details about the **Characters** and their **Problem**. Add some or all of the dialogue from page 79 to spice up your story. Finish the story by **Solving** the problem.

_____

_____

_____

_____

_____

_____

_____

_____

_____

Did you know . . .

stories have five essential elements?

1. *Characters*

2. *Setting*

3. *Plot*

4. *Conflict*

5. *Resolution*

_____

_____

_____

_____

_____

_____

_____

_____

 GO TO NEXT PAGE ➡

_____

_____

_____

_____

_____

_____

_____

_____

_____

_____

_____

_____

_____

_____

_____

_____

_____

_____

_____

_____

_____

_____

What would be a great title for this story? Write your title here. ↙

_____

 GO TO NEXT PAGE ➡

Illustrate your story.

Beginning

Middle

End

 GO TO NEXT PAGE ➡

What else could happen to the characters?

Other story ideas

STOP

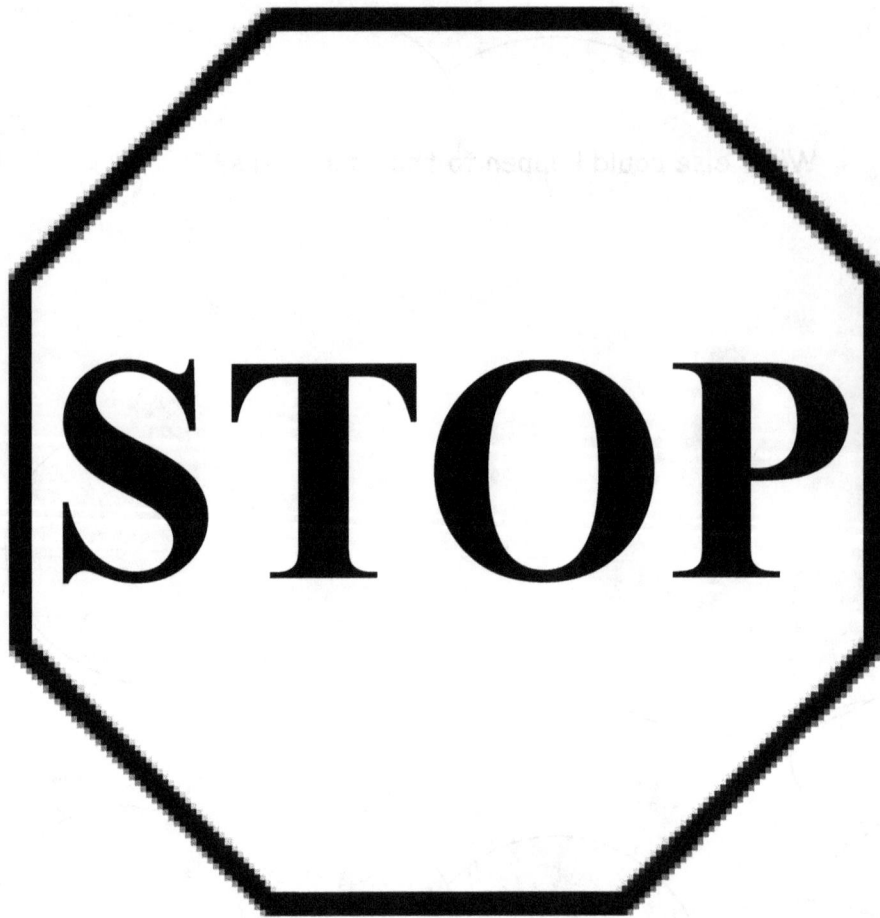

CONGRATULATIONS!

You have just finished writing Chapter 8

Now . . .

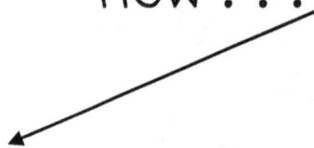

Go back to page 75. **Write the title of this story** on the line next to TITLE: _____. Then **write your name** next to WRITTEN BY: _____ and ILLUSTRATED BY: _____. Draw a picture in the box above the title that will show the reader what this chapter is about.

After you finish page 75, start the next chapter

GO TO NEXT PAGE ➔

CHAPTER 9

TITLE:_____

_____

WRITTEN BY: _____

ILLUSTRATED BY: _____

86

Draw your own picture —or— choose a photograph from your phone or computer and print it —or— CUT A PICTURE FROM A MAGAZINE, NEWSPAPER, OR TRAVEL BROCHURE, **and glue or tape it into the box.**

Fill in the blanks. Write an answer to each prompt.

1. Get your senses involved. **Look at the picture.** Write down what you **See:** colors, shapes, sizes, people, and things. _____

_____

Put yourself in the picture.

Write down what you might **Hear:** _____ **Smell:** _____

Touch: _____ **Taste:** _____

I CAN'T THINK OF ANYTHING TO WRITE! Don't panic. **Help is on the next page** ⟶

2. Where is this place? Is it real or imaginary? **Location:** _____

3. When does this picture take place? **Time Period:** _____

4. What kind of day is it? **Weather:** _____

5. How does this picture make you feel? **Emotion:** _____

6. **Create** two **Characters**. Use the prompts to describe each one.

Character #1 Decide if your character will be a person, animal, or thing.

Body Frame: _____ Hair: _____

Eyes: _____ Complexion (face): _____

Teeth: _____ Nose: _____ Clothing: _____

_____

Personality: _____

Name: _____

GO TO NEXT PAGE ⟶

CHAPTER 9

TITLE:_____

_____

WRITTEN BY: _____

ILLUSTRATED BY: _____

86

Draw your own picture —or— choose a photograph from your phone or computer and print it —or— cut A PICTURE FROM A MAGAZINE, NEWSPAPER, OR TRAVEL BROCHURE, **and glue or tape it into the box.**

Fill in the blanks. Write an answer to each prompt.

1. Get your senses involved. **Look at the picture.** Write down what you **See:** colors, shapes, sizes, people, and things. _____

_____

Put yourself in the picture.

Write down what you might **Hear:** _____ **Smell:** _____

Touch: _____ **Taste:** _____

I CAN'T THINK OF ANYTHING TO WRITE! Don't panic. **Help is on the next page** ⟶

2. Where is this place? Is it real or imaginary? **Location:** _____

3. When does this picture take place? **Time Period:** _____

4. What kind of day is it? **Weather:** _____

5. How does this picture make you feel? **Emotion:** _____

6. **Create** two **Characters.** Use the prompts to describe each one.

Character #1 Decide if your character will be a person, animal, or thing.

Body Frame: _____ Hair: _____

Eyes: _____ Complexion (face): _____

Teeth: _____ Nose: _____ Clothing: _____

_____

Personality: _____

Name: _____

GO TO NEXT PAGE ➡

Character #2 <u>Decide if your character will be a person, animal, or thing.</u>

Body Frame: _____ Hair: _____

Eyes: _____ Complexion (face): _____

Teeth: _____ Nose: _____ Clothing: _____

_____

Personality: _____

Name: _____

7. Make up a **Problem** within the picture. What is the problem? What is happening to the

characters? _____

_____

8. What is the **Solution** to the problem? _____

_____

Need Help? Use a *Jump Starter* word, if needed, to respond to the prompts.	Oops! I want to use one of the words, but I don't know what it means. Write the word you want to use. Look up the word in the dictionary and write down what it means.
Hear: applause	_____
Smell: soap	_____
Touch: phone screen	_____
Taste: toothpaste	_____
Location: cave	_____
Time Period: Sunday	_____
Weather: pollution	_____
Emotion: pleased	_____
Body Frame: key, marshmallow	_____
Hair: Beehive, French twist	_____
Eyes: anxious, passionate	_____
Complexion (face): radiating, yellow	_____
Teeth: grimy, metal braces	_____
Nose: red, cold	_____
Clothing: costume, dirty socks	_____
Personality: condescending, meddlesome	_____
Problem: Jellyfish pulling you out to sea	

GO TO NEXT PAGE ▰

88

Draw your characters.

Character #1

Character #2

 GO TO NEXT PAGE ➡

Write dialogue between your characters. What are they saying to each other?
<u>Write one sentence in each speech bubble.</u> See page 96 for examples of dialogue.

Character #1

Character #2

Character #1

Character #2

Character #1

Character #2

Character #1

Character #2

Character #1

Character #2

 GO TO NEXT PAGE

90

Put it all together. Use your writing from pages 86-89 to write a short story. Describe the **Location**, **Time Period**, and **Weather**. Add details about the **Characters** and their **Problem**. Add some or all of the dialogue from page 89 to spice up your story. Finish the story by **Solving** the problem.

_____

_____

_____

_____

_____

_____

_____

_____

_____

Did you know . . .

stories should answer the Five Ws?

<u>Who?</u> (are the characters)

<u>What?</u> (are they doing)

<u>Where?</u> (is this happening)

<u>When?</u> (does it take place)

<u>Why?</u> (did it happen)

_____

_____

_____

_____

_____

_____

_____

_____

_____

_____

_____

 GO TO NEXT PAGE ➡

_____

_____

_____

_____

_____

_____

_____

_____

_____

_____

_____

_____

_____

_____

_____

_____

_____

_____

What would be a great title for this story? Write your title here.

_____

 GO TO NEXT PAGE

Illustrate your story.

Beginning

Middle

End

 GO TO NEXT PAGE ➡

STOP

CONGRATULATIONS!

You have just finished writing Chapter 9

Now . . .

Go back to page 85. **Write the title of this story** on the line next to TITLE: _____. Then **write your name** next to WRITTEN BY: _____ and ILLUSTRATED BY: _____. Draw a picture in the box above the title that will show the reader what this chapter is about.

<u>After</u> you finish page 85, go to page 94 and write about you, the author of this book.

GO TO NEXT PAGE ➡

Write about the person who wrote this book-your name, things you like to do, where you live, pets, family, friends, anything you want the reader to know about you. Tape or glue a picture of the author into the square.

About the Author

_____

_____

_____

_____

_____

_____

_____

Comments: What I like best about this book is . . .

_____

_____

_____

_____

_____

 GO TO NEXT PAGE ➡

Create a list of your own **Jump Starter** words.

_____   _____

_____   _____

_____   _____

_____   _____

_____   _____

_____   _____

_____   _____

_____   _____

_____   _____

_____   _____

_____   _____

_____   _____

_____   _____

_____   _____

_____   _____

_____   _____

_____   _____

 GO TO NEXT PAGE ➡

96

Use exciting action words with your dialogue.

admitted	giggled	mashed	sang
advised	grumbled	measured	scolded
announced	growled	melted	screamed
answered	grunted	moaned	shouted
argued	gulped	mocked	shrieked
babbled	hissed	moped	sighed
barked	hooted	muddled along	sniveled
begged	hollered	murmured	stammered
boasted	held	nagged	stomped
boomed	hooked	nailed	tattled
bragged	hunted	nodded off	taunted
cackled	insisted	noted	teased
chattered	interrupted	observed	urged
chirped	irritated	offered	used up
chuckled	itched	opened	ushered
complained	introduced	opposed	vacuumed
coughed	investigated	ordered	ventured
demanded	jabbered	pestered	voiced
denied	joked	pleaded	wailed
discovered	jumped in	prattled	whimpered
disputed	jumped off	preached	whined
dreamed	jumped on	professed	whispered
echoed	kicked	quarreled	whistled
examined	knocked	questioned	x-rayed
exhausted	keeled over	quit	yapped
explained	lectured	quizzed	yelped
finished	lied	rambled	zipped
fished	landed	ranted	zoomed
followed	lapped	refused	
frightened	lashed out	roared	
fumed	latched onto	robbed	
fussed	left		

Example: Stewart inched his way toward the entrance of the dark cave.

Character #1
Peering inside he whispered, "Anyone in there?"

Character #2
"Go AWAY!" roared a voice from inside the dark hole.

Character #1
Shaking in his boots, Stewart stammered, "Is . . . is . . . my baseball in there?" He shouted, "I'm coming in RIGHT NOW!"

Character #2
"I'm coming in RIGHT NOW!" echoed back to him.

Character #1
Tripping over a rock, Stewart stumbled into the cave, "Please don't hurt me!" he whimpered.

Character #2
"Hmmmm. What have we here?"

 GO TO NEXT PAGE ➡

Dear Writer,

I believe every person has a story within. It doesn't matter if you are 5 or 105, everyone has a story to tell. Writing in the Rough, LLC was formed with the belief that you can create a story if given a few writing prompts.

Jump Starter words are random and will hopefully create curiosity, "Hey, what does that word really mean?" By looking up the words, the writer will learn new vocabulary. Use the five Ws (who, what, where, when, and why) to expand the Jump Starter words. For example: Who is worried? What happened in Outer Space? Where is the solar eclipse? When did the character get his head shaved? Why did he get his head shaved? Ask some how questions. How did the dental floss taste? How are you going to keep the snooping character out of your business?

This is rough draft writing so don't worry about grammar, punctuation, or spelling. The purpose of this book is to inspire writers to write. Let your imagination loose, pick up your pen, and start writing today.

Need Help?
Use a Jump Starter word, if needed, to respond to the prompts.

Hear: pounding
Smell: cheese
Touch: flour
Taste: dental floss
Location: Outer Space
Time Period: Stone Age
Weather: solar eclipse
Emotion: blissful
Body Frame: tree, muscular
Hair: Ducktail, shaved
Eyes: stunned, worried
Complexion (face): wrinkles, mole
Teeth: squeaky-clean, stained
Nose: aquiline, snub-nosed
Clothing: mask, jacket
Personality: live wire, snooping
Problem: collapsed bridge

ACKNOWLEDGEMENTS

Thank you Christopher Ulbrich and Lynn Gallagher for your editing suggestions!

A special thanks to Charlene Carpenter (www.CharleneCarpenter.com) for your eagle eyes! I could not have done this without your help. Thank you friend!

I would love to hear about your writing adventures.
You can email me: Jan@writingintherough.com
Or visit me at: www.writingintherough.com

Best Wishes! Jan LaFave

Use the blank pages to write and draw ideas for your next book.